How to Make

FIRST-CLASS CARDS

How to Make
FIRST-CLASS CARDS

Debbie Brown

GUILD OF MASTER CRAFTSMAN PUBLICATIONS

First published 2001 by
Guild of Master Craftsman Publications Ltd,
166 High Street, Lewes,
East Sussex BN7 1XU
Copyright © GMC Publications Ltd 2001
Text & card designs © Debbie Brown 2001

ISBN 1 86108 210 X

A catalogue record of this book is available from the British Library.

Editor: Nicola Wright
Designer: Danny McBride
Photographer: Anthony Bailey
Typeface: Rotis & Jacoby
Colour separation: Viscan Graphics (Singapore)
Printed and bound by Kyodo Printing (Singapore)
under the supervision of MRM Graphics,
Winslow, Buckinghamshire, UK

10 9 8 7 6 5 4 3 2 1

CONTENTS

DEDICATION

With love to my husband Pete,
without whose help this book would
never have been written, and to
my children, Sam and Katie.

ACKNOWLEDGEMENTS

My husband, Pete, for your endless help and patience. Steve 'Spike' Brown at Blue Feather Photography, for your usual first-class photographs. Craft Creations Ltd, Chesthunt, Herts, for your friendly and efficient service across the years. Greg Hill, for all your advice and encouragement. My editor, Nicola Wright, for helping me with my first book and for the use of your hands for the photographs!

INTRODUCTION

Card making is a very rewarding and inexpensive hobby. It requires no specialist equipment, no dedicated workspace, and no specialist skills or artistic training and it gives the satisfaction of making something yourself, in a relatively short space of time, and much cheaper than it can be bought in the shops. All these things make it the perfect pastime. Card making is a hobby that can be enjoyed by people of all ages and abilities, and one that will give as much pleasure to those who receive the cards as it does to those who make them.

With all these points in mind, my aim has been to create a book of sophisticated designs which are suitable for all tastes and occasions, and which will prove that you don't need to be an artist, or spend a fortune, to produce attractive, professional-looking cards. The designs range from those taking only a matter of minutes to complete, to ones which will need a little longer and I have given estimates as to how long each one is likely to take. As you can see, a lot can be achieved even if you only have the odd half an hour to spare now and then. The instructions are laid out in clear, easy to follow stages and there are lots of tips throughout. You will find advice on equipment, materials, and basic techniques, as well as suggestions on where to look for inspiration for creating your own designs.

It is always nice to receive a personal, tailor-made card, and it conveys so much more thought than buying one off the shelf. It is something that will always be remembered, and unlike many shop bought ones that will be thrown away or recycled, it will be kept and treasured long after the occasion has passed.

Cards can be given for all sorts of reasons, not just for birthdays and Christmas. They can be used to say anything from 'let's get together for lunch', 'sorry I missed you' or even just to say 'hello', and they have distinct advantages over a telephone call. They allow you time to compose exactly what you want to say, with nothing forgotten, and with special thoughts that can be read and enjoyed many times over, by those who receive them.

For those of you who are new to the craft, I hope that by following the advice in the next few chapters and trying your hand at some of the designs, you will gain the confidence and the inspiration to start designing and making your own first-class cards.

CHAPTER 1

Paper

The main material used in each of the projects in this book is paper. It is one of the most versatile materials ever invented and we are surrounded by paper products every day, ranging from absorbent tissue papers, newspapers and writing papers, through to packaging materials and even roofing paper used in building construction. It is cheap, easy to work with and available in a huge range of colours, weights, textures and finishes, and this makes it ideal for use in many crafts.

If you pay a visit to a good art and craft shop or stationers, you will be able to see many of the different types of paper on offer, including foils, gloss and matt finish, marbled, parchment, graduated and rainbow, embossed, corrugated, textured and handmade, and when you begin designing your own cards you will find it useful to start building up a collection of these. If you plan to make a lot of cards, it may be worth contacting your local mail-order paper and card suppliers as they can be cheaper if you are buying larger quantities.

Corrugated foil-coated papers

It isn't always necessary to buy pretty papers as there are plenty available for free too. Before you throw anything away, look to see if there is any paper or card that could be saved for use in future designs, such as giftwrap, packaging, paper bags, left over wallpaper, and tissue paper. Some envelopes have attractive patterns printed on the inside, so you might be able to put some of your junk mail to good use and help the environment at the same time.

I have only listed a few types from the enormous range available. You will undoubtedly find many more, and it will not be difficult to gather together a very attractive and inspiring selection.

Printed 3D-effect paper in various colours

A BRIEF HISTORY OF PAPER

Today, with its abundant supply and low prices, most of us take paper for granted, but this hasn't always been the case. For centuries paper was expensive, and therefore only available to the few who could afford it, and being made by hand, supply was limited. It has only been due to the huge advances in technology over the last two hundred years that we now treat it as a throw-away product.

More than 5000 years ago, the Egyptians made a type of paper using the pith from papyrus reeds. This was woven into a mat and then pounded into flat sheets, which they could then write on, and examples of these can still be seen in some museums. Paper, as we know it today, is generally thought to have been invented by a Chinese court official named Ts'ai Lun in AD 105. At first he used ropes and old fishing nets before moving on to plant fibres and silk threads to make his paper.

Metallic, mirror and holographic papers

The art of paper making was kept a secret for hundreds of years, and it is thought the Japanese started making their first paper in the seventh century using mulberry bark. In AD 751 the Arabs captured some Chinese prisoners at Samarkand, some of whom were skilled in the art of paper making. They were forced by their captors to teach them the process, and with its large supply of raw materials, Samarkand soon became the paper-making centre of the Arab world. The paper produced here was made mainly from flax, hemp and linen rags.

From Samarkand, knowledge of the craft spread westward, and with the Moorish invasion of Spain, paper making was introduced to Europe. Within a few hundred years, paper mills had been built in most European countries, and the paper they produced was also made mainly from flax, hemp and rags.

As the centuries passed, demand for paper increased dramatically, but it was all still made by hand. To produce the quantities required, the process needed to be automated, and the first successful paper-making machine was built in 1803 by the Fourdrinier brothers (Henry and Sealy), and Bryan Donkin.

As demand continued to grow, raw materials became scarce, and it was only possible to produce paper on a large scale when wood pulp was introduced as a source during the nineteenth century, and this, in turn, led to the development of larger and faster paper-making machines. Paper mills today continue to use wood pulp in the manufacturing process along with large amounts of recycled paper.

MACHINE-MADE PAPERS

The majority of all paper and card is made by machine and it is usually manufactured in one continuous process. The pulp is poured onto a moving belt, which then passes through a series of rollers and driers until the end product, a large reel of paper, is produced. This can then be cut and finished depending on its intended use. It is generally less expensive than handmade paper due

A colourful array of machine-made papers

to the vast quantities manufactured, and in the main, the designs in this book are constructed from machine-made paper and card.

GRAIN

All machine-made papers have a grain. This is the term used to describe the direction in which the fibres in the paper lie. The pulp fibres settle in the same direction as the movement of the belt on which the paper was made and the paper will fold, tear and crease more easily with the grain than against it, so it is always a good idea to check for this, before using any of these techniques. One way to find out which way the grain runs is to gently flex the sheet between your hands in both directions, it will flex more easily along its grain. Another method is to tear two strips from the sheet, one in each direction, the torn edge will be straighter along the grain than the one torn across it.

Mulberry paper is made from the bark of the mulberry tree

WEIGHT

It is a good idea when designing your own cards to know a little bit about weight and thickness, as this will allow you to pick the most suitable paper or card for your application. This is especially important if you are buying mail order where you may not be able to see the paper before you buy it, although most good companies will send you sample swatches if you ask. Paper is usually measured in grams per square metre, abbreviated to 'g/m^2' or 'gsm', so a piece of 100gsm paper measuring 1m x 1m weighs 100g. As a guide, tissue papers weigh about 18gsm, general writing and photocopy papers weigh between 80gsm and 120gsm, and the more heavyweight papers between 150gsm and 200gsm. Paper weighing more than 225gsm is classed as card. Another abbreviation used when describing paper and card is 'mic'. This is short for microns and indicates its thickness. 1000mic equals 1mm.

A selection of differently finished machine-made papers including foil embossed and rainbow

SIZING

This is the term used to describe the coating given to paper and card to make it less absorbent. It is a glue-like substance, usually gelatine or starch, that may be added to both machine-made and handmade papers so that ink and paint will not bleed into them.

HANDMADE PAPERS

A selection of specialist papers including Japanese lace

Handmade papers have no grain as the fibres settle in all directions when they are made. Some have glitter, flower petals, silk threads, grass or other items incorporated into them, whilst some of the oriental papers have the appearance of lace, and can look, and feel, beautiful. They are a bit more expensive than other types of paper but are well worth the extra, as you only need a small amount to add a touch of sophistication to your designs.

TRACING PAPER

For most of the projects in this book you will need to trace and transfer some, or all, of the design. Tracing paper is readily available from stationers, office suppliers and art shops, but for a cheaper alternative, I have found kitchen greaseproof paper to be a good substitute in most cases.

STORING PAPER

The way you store your paper will largely depend on the quantities involved, but in all cases it should be stored flat if at all possible. For smaller amounts you could use a large envelope or make a portfolio by sandwiching the paper between two sheets of strong card and tying with tapes or string. For larger quantities a spare draw would be ideal but if, like me, you don't have one, you could use a large, shallow cardboard box (the type used for apples can accommodate fairly large sheets and lots of them, and you should be able to pick one up at your local supermarket). If you do have to roll your paper, be sure to do this quite loosely, as this avoids it developing a permanent curl.

Paper

GREETINGS CARD BLANKS

All of the cards on the following pages were made using
ready-cut greetings card blanks. I prefer to use these as it
can be quite difficult and time consuming to achieve the same
level of accuracy when making your own, especially when
cutting apertures, and ready-cut blanks give guaranteed results
every time. They are not expensive and are available in a wide
range of colours, sizes and finishes from art and craft shops,
haberdashery departments and specialist mail-order suppliers. If
you wish to make your own, see the chapter on Basic Techniques
on page 27.

A selection of handmade
papers

Ready-cut card blanks

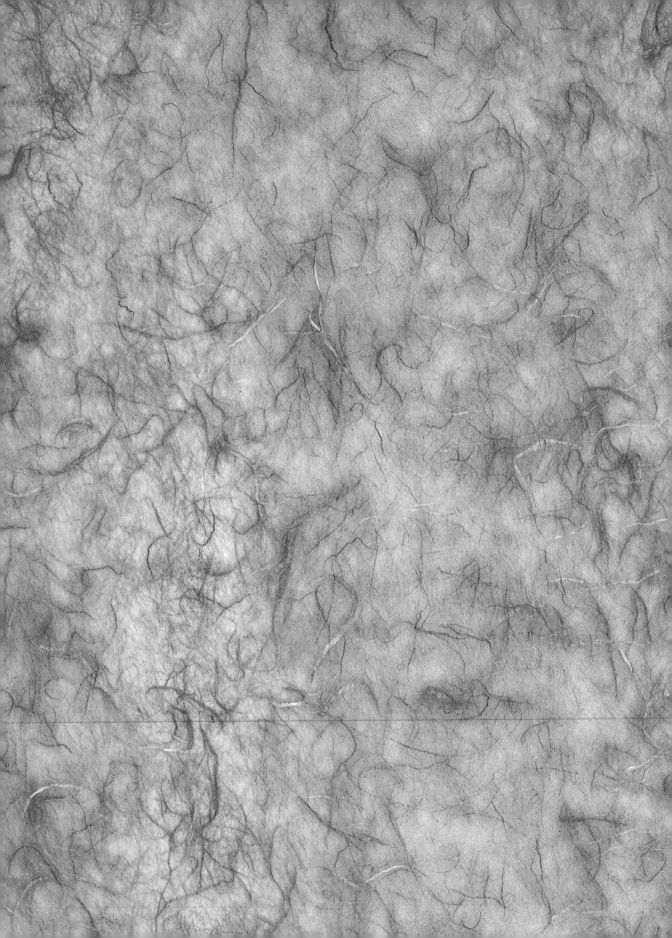

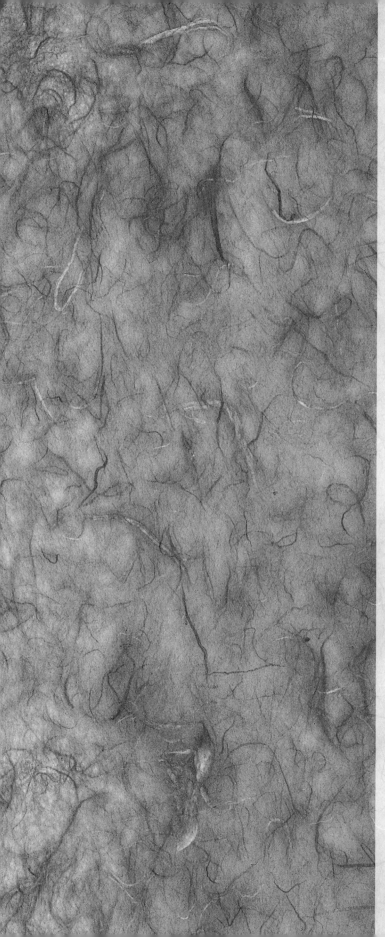

CHAPTER 2

Equipment

One of the handy things about card making is that it requires no specialist equipment to get started. In fact, you will probably already have most, or all, of the basic items needed.

I have divided the equipment list into two parts, with the first being those items which I feel are essential. As you can see, it is a short list and this really is all you need to begin this very rewarding hobby. If you are using ready-cut blanks, all of the designs in this book can be completed using this basic equipment, but if you are making your own mounts, you may need a craft knife and steel rule.

The second and slightly longer list, is of equipment that you may find useful especially when designing your own cards. None of these items are essential, but they can help to either add interest or give a more professional finish to your work.

ESSENTIAL

Scissors For general use an average-sized, sharp pair of scissors with pointed blades will be perfectly adequate but you may also find a pair of embroidery scissors useful for cutting small shapes or awkward corners. Above all, they should be comfortable to use. If all of your scissors at home are blunt, rusty or otherwise unsuitable, it would be advisable to invest in a new pair, as you will probably use these more than any other tool.

Drawing Equipment An HB pencil for general use and a white pencil for use on dark coloured paper and card. A pencil sharpener and an eraser. A ruler for drawing straight lines and a set square for accurate corners. A fine-tipped black pen, and gold/silver metallic pens for adding small details. If you use handmade mulberry paper on your cards you will also need a small, inexpensive paintbrush for applying water (see chapter on Basic Techniques for instructions on the edging method).

Tweezers Essential for holding, positioning and arranging small items. I find pointed tweezers much more versatile than flat-ended ones for precise work.

TIP
To reduce the risk of accidents always use a sharp blade, and when cutting through thick card make several gentler cuts rather than trying to go through in one go. If you have a scalpel without a blade cover, store it with the blade embedded into an old wine bottle cork.

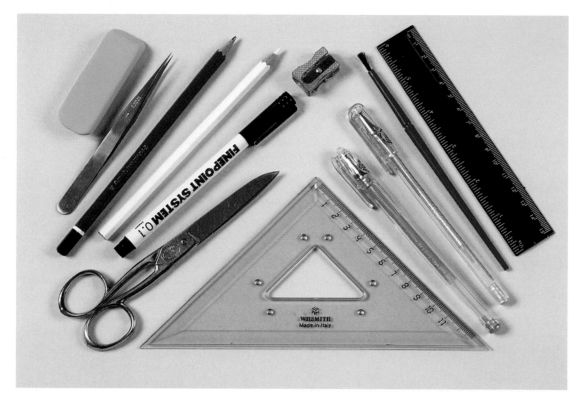

Once you have collected together your basic equipment you may find it helpful to keep it all in a box or tin. You will then have everything you need in one place and readily to hand for your projects.

Essential equipment

USEFUL

Paper Trimmer These are very useful pieces of equipment and I personally wouldn't be without one. They give a quick, clean, straight cut (which is something I find difficult to achieve by hand and I will only use a scalpel if it is absolutely necessary). They are available in a range of sizes for home use but I find the small 22cm (8½in) size perfectly adequate.

Craft Knife or Scalpel These can be used for cutting straight lines and for scoring thicker card for folding. They can also be useful when cutting small details which would be difficult to reach with scissors.

TIP
For accuracy always use a sharp pencil.

13

Useful equipment

Steel Rule Always use a steel rule when cutting or scoring straight lines with a scalpel or craft knife as the blade could snag in a plastic or wooden one. Some steel rules have finger guards for added protection.

Cutting Mat Whenever you use a craft knife or scalpel you must protect your work surface. If, like me, you rarely use a knife, you can improvise with a piece of thick cardboard, but if you think you may use one frequently it might be worth buying a self-healing cutting mat.

Decorative Edging Scissors Gone are the days when the only fancy edging you could achieve easily was a zigzag using pinking shears. With the scissors available today, you can produce a wide variety of attractive edging which can add interest to your work, including 'deckle edge', 'waves', 'scallops', and even ones to create your own postage stamp-type edges. Corner-cutting scissors are also available, again in a broad range, and these are used to create interesting decorative corners quickly and easily.

Hole Punch This can be useful when making gift tags, or as a quick method of producing lots of small circles to decorate your cards – falling snow for instance.

Decorative Punches These are available in a multitude of designs and produce small, perfectly cut shapes that would be too difficult to do by hand. These include designs of cats, stars, teddy bears, feet, suns and dolphins to name but a few and they are ideal for adding surface decoration to your cards.

SAFETY
As with all cutting equipment, things with sharp points and heat-generating equipment, care must be taken whilst using them. Always follow the manufacturers' instructions and never leave them unattended where children could pick them up.

Decorative punches, stamps and scissors

Glue Gun This piece of equipment is used to turn solid sticks of glue into a liquid adhesive. The sticks are fed into the gun which then melts them. There are different sizes and styles available, some of which operate when you squeeze a trigger and some which require you to push the glue stick in with your finger. I would recommend getting one with a trigger if at all possible as these give you more control over how much glue is released. To use these guns you will also need to work within reach of a power point. Take care not to touch the hot glue as it can blister or burn your skin.

CHAPTER 3

Adhesives

To construct the cards featured in this book I have used three main types of adhesive. All-purpose craft glue, spray adhesive and hot-melt glue (glue gun). Each have their own properties which make them more suitable for certain types of applications.

All-purpose craft glue This is my favourite adhesive and I use it for almost everything. It is suitable for sticking paper, card, fabric and trimmings such as ribbons, bows, beads, sequins and feathers. It is applied by squeezing straight from the bottle so it is clean and easy to use, and it is also transparent when dry.

Spray adhesive This is a solvent-based glue supplied in aerosol form. It has some advantages over other types of glue in that it gives an even coverage and is non-wrinkling, which is very useful on thin papers and foil, where blobs of glue could show up as lumps on the finished work. It also allows for repositioning and the excess glue can be cleaned off with lighter fluid. Even with these advantages though, I only use it when I have to as it is quite messy and not particularly easy to use. Because it is a solvent-based spray, it must be used in a well-ventilated area, and the mist does have a tendency to spread, so work surfaces need to be well protected. One way of doing this is to make a spray booth. This may sound a bit complicated but it is quite simply a medium-sized cardboard box, turned on its side, with several layers of scrap paper in the bottom. The top sheet can then be removed after each use leaving a clean one for next time.

Adhesives l to r – spray adhesive, all-purpose craft glue, hot-melt glue and gun

Hot-melt glue This is applied with a glue gun which melts the solid glue sticks to give a liquid adhesive. You need to work quite quickly with this

glue as it starts to harden again in a matter of seconds. However, this can be a useful property when it comes to sticking fairly bulky items like dried and silk flowers, baskets and mushrooms. All-purpose craft glue will stick these, but you would need to hold them in position or weight them down for a while. Care must be taken when using a glue gun as both the gun and the liquid glue become very hot.

TIP
Add decorative glue last as it takes a while to dry. This will avoid the risk of smudging it whilst working on the rest of your card.

Decorative glues These can be useful for adding decorative detail to your work. They are available in a range of finishes including glitter and glow-in-the-dark, and are usually applied by squeezing straight from the tube which makes them quick, easy and clean to work with. If you are using these for the first time, it is a good idea to practise on scraps of paper first until you get the required pressure right. Glitter glue can be added wherever you want a bit of sparkle, the glue dries transparent leaving the glitter stuck to the card. I often use this for outlines, dots and other fine details, but I have found it wrinkles the paper slightly if it is used over large areas. Glow-

Decorative glitter glues add sparkle to your cards

in-the-dark glue is particularly popular with children and I have yet to meet one who isn't fascinated with this novelty. It can give hours of fun and will probably mean that your card will still be in use long after the occasion has passed. Like glitter glue, this glue tends to work best when used for highlighting details and outlines.

Whichever adhesives you choose to use, read and follow the manufacturers instructions for application and safety. I would also recommend testing any glue you haven't used before on scraps to familiarize yourself with its characteristics.

CHAPTER 4

Materials

When you start making and designing your own cards, you will need a selection of items for surface decoration. This chapter offers suggestions on some of the things you could use, and where you might find them.

WHAT TO BUY AND WHERE TO LOOK

Art and craft shops and haberdashery departments offer an extensive range of suitable, reasonably priced materials including ribbons, buttons, bows, beads, sequins, feathers, pompoms, coloured pipe cleaners, lace, peel offs, stick-on eyes, diamantés, glitter glue and fabric paint.

Florists can be a good source for all manner of useful materials, not just the obvious things like dried and silk flowers, but also small wicker baskets and hats, tiny teddies, small pots and many types of lightweight polystyrene and paper items, like the seahorse and mushrooms featured later.

Market stalls are another good source of varied and cheap materials and in some cases offer goods in smaller quantities than are available elsewhere.

Bric-a-brac stalls and jumble sales are also ideal places for cheap materials. You can find beads, braid, buttons, jewellery, and many other interesting and unusual pieces. If you are looking for dried or silk flowers, you can pick up a single flower arrangement cheaply giving a nice mix, rather than buying a whole bunch of each flower needed.

There are also many other outlets worth investigating when you are looking for both materials and inspiration for your designs.

Many of the accessories available for dolls' houses are ideal for use on cards as they are small and lightweight. Similarly, hobby and model train suppliers stock items used for scenery etc. that can be adapted for use in your designs.

Artificial plants, gravel and other interesting odds and ends can be found in aquatic/pet shops, and suppliers of cake decorating materials stock many accessories perfectly suited to card making.

Specialist bead shops are also worth a look as they stock beads in almost every colour, shape and size imaginable, any one of which might add the finishing touch to your work. In fact, almost anything that is small enough, not too heavy, and can be affixed to a card can be considered for use in a design.

Decorative materials

THINGS FOR FREE

As card making uses very small amounts of materials, it is a great way of using up lots of things that would normally be thrown away. I have already mentioned paper and card but there are many other items that can be salvaged for use in your designs. Leftovers from sewing projects including small pieces of ribbon, scraps of fabric, thread, wool and odd buttons are all worth keeping. Other items worth saving are cellophane and ribbons from bouquets, decorative postage stamps, net from washing tablet and orange bags, clean serviettes and doillies. Chocolate boxes are very recyclable, you can use the acetate lids, ribbons, bows, metallic card and even the sweet wrappers. I could go on but I'm sure once you start looking at things with card-making potential in mind, you will begin to find many more things for yourself.

Recycled materials

READY-MADE PRODUCTS

When looking for inspiration for your own designs, it is worth checking out some of the many products that you can use on paper and card to give interesting effects, like the decorative glues mentioned in the chapter on adhesives.

Some types of fabric paint work well and can be used to produce raised outlines and details as they retain their shape when they are dry. Liquid appliqué can give very pleasing and unusual results. It looks a little like paint and is applied by squeezing straight from the tube, but when it is dry and then heated with a hair dryer, it puffs up like a soufflé.

There is also a seemingly endless range of pens, paints, inks and crayons available that can be used to produce attractive finishes, and you don't have to be an artist to use them. Paints can be used to create interesting backgrounds by sponging, stippling, spattering and stenciling, using one or more colours, and in finishes such as metallic, pearl and fluorescent. Gel pens are a favourite of mine and give a thin line of vibrant colour, the metallic and creamy pastel ones work well on dark coloured paper and card. Even the humble wax crayon can be used to good effect for resist painting or blending.

With so many products available, my advice is to experiment, it's great fun and you are bound to come up with something you like, or get results that will inspire you in new directions. Try to spend some time in your local art and craft shops researching the materials and products available, and if you have any questions, either ask in the shop, or telephone the manufacturer, I have always found them to be very helpful.

With so much to choose from, the design possibilities are endless, and your creations can be as simple, or extravagant, as you choose to make them.

CHAPTER 5

Basic
Techniques

FOLDING PAPER AND CARD

Some of the more lightweight papers can be folded quite easily by hand, but if the same is done with more heavyweight paper or card, the fold is likely to be uneven or broken, so a little help is needed to achieve a crisp finish. This can be done by creasing or scoring. A common mistake is to do this on the wrong side of the card, this should always be done on the side of the material which will be stretched when it is folded over.

CREASING

This method is used to create a small indent in the paper or card to make folding easier. Place a ruler or other straight edge along the fold line and run a pointed, but blunt, tool along the edge. You could use a knitting needle or the back edge of a pair of scissors. This will leave an indent ready to fold. This method is suitable for the majority of the paper and card you are likely to use when making greetings cards.

Creasing method

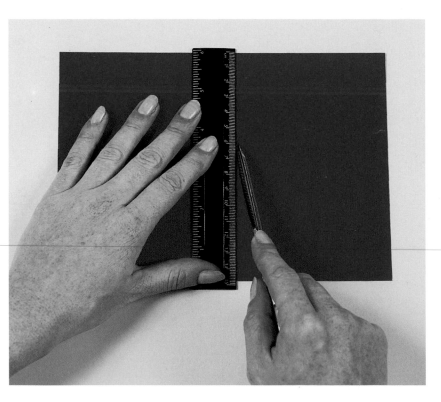

SCORING

This method produces very crisp folds and is useful when working with more heavyweight card where creasing would not be sufficient. The surface of the card is cut which makes folding very easy. Place a steel rule along the fold line and hold down firmly. Gently run the back edge of a craft knife or a scissor blade along the edge to cut through only the very surface of the card. Care must be taken not to cut too deeply and it is often a good idea to practice on some waste scraps first until you are confident that you are using the right pressure.

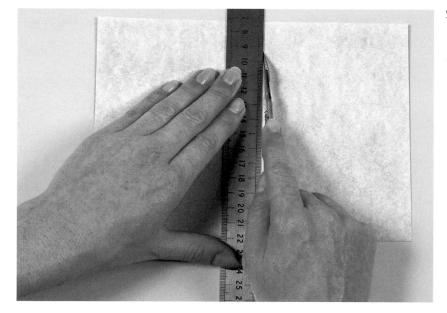

Scoring method

TRACING

To reproduce most of my designs, you will need to trace the templates which can be found at the back of the book in Chapter 9 (see pages 116–119). They are shown actual size and right side up. Lay the tracing paper over the template and with a pencil, draw round the outline. Turn the tracing paper over and lay it on the wrong side of your chosen paper. Draw round the shape again and this will leave a faint outline ready for you to cut out. To trace onto black or very dark paper follow the same procedure, but using a white pencil instead.

USING DOUBLE-SIDED FOAM PADS (STICKY FIXERS)

For some of the designs using aperture cards, I have recommended
securing the front flap to the inside using double-sided foam pads.
This is not essential, you could glue the flaps shut, but using them
helps to give depth to the finished card. If you wish to use this
method, cut a foam pad into several smaller pieces, stick three or
four of these pieces to the inside, long edge of the front flap,
making sure that you place them close to the edge so that they do
not show from the front when it is closed. It is advisable to check
for this before finally closing the flap so that they can be carefully
removed if they are in the wrong place. Foam pads can also be
used to add depth within the design itself, but again, make sure
that they are hidden from view.

Using double-sided
foam pads

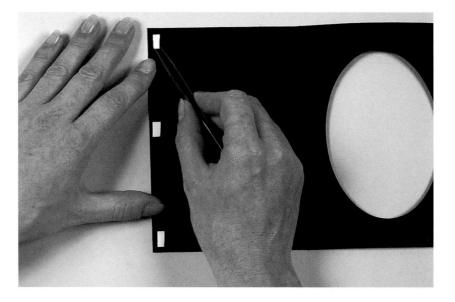

EDGING HANDMADE MULBERRY PAPER

The long fibres in mulberry paper are very attractive and it is ideal
for adding a touch of sophistication to handmade cards, but this
effect is almost completely lost if it is cut with scissors. To achieve
the delicate, wispy edges, you will need a small paintbrush and
some water. Draw your required outline with a wet paintbrush, then
gently pull the paper apart along these lines, the fibres will
separate, giving it its characteristic edge.

Edging handmade
mulberry paper

MAKING YOUR OWN CARD MOUNTS

As I mentioned in the chapter on paper, I prefer to use ready-cut
card blanks and I have always managed to find the right card for
my needs. But there may be occasions when you need a certain
shape, size or colour not offered by the supplier, or you may just
prefer to make your own. The two most useful mounts to know
how to make are single-fold and double-fold or three-panel cards.

Single-fold is the simplest, and as the name suggests, it is basically
a piece of card folded in half.

Double-fold or three-panel cards are a little more complex, but a
lot more versatile, and if you want to mount your design behind an
aperture, this is the type you will need. They can also be useful if
you want to sew directly onto the card, or use studs or any other
items that require you to pierce through the card, as the front flap
can be secured to the inside to hide any loose ends etc.

To make a basic rectangular, double-fold mount, first decide what size you want the finished card to be. Using these measurements, cut a piece of card 1 x height and 3 x width (see diagram below).

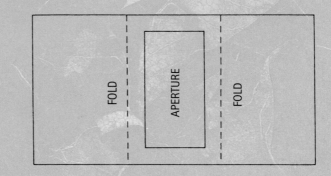

Divide the longest edge into three and crease or score two fold lines to give three equal panels. If you want an aperture, cut this from the centre panel. Rectangles and squares are the easiest but you could experiment with all sorts of interesting shapes.

When you are ready to assemble your card, fold the right hand flap in and secure. You may need to trim the edge slightly so that it fits neatly inside.

This basic method could be adapted to produce cards of any shape, as long as each panel is joined along the fold lines, you could try circles, octagons, stars or anything else that takes your fancy.

ENVELOPES AND BOXES

Once you have finished your card, you will need something to put it in. Whether this is an envelope, or a box, will depend on the depth of the design, and also whether you are posting it, or delivering it by hand. If you are sending it by mail, most of the flatter designs should be fine in an envelope, although you may like to put bubble wrap around any raised items for added protection, but for the deeper, more fragile designs, I would advise putting them in a box.

After all the care that has gone into your creation, you don't want it ruined in the post. If you are delivering it by hand, it probably won't require quite the same level of protection.

ENVELOPES

Envelopes are available in a wide range of sizes and colours from stationers, department stores, art and craft shops, and mail order from suppliers of greetings card blanks, so if you do not wish to make your own, it should be fairly easy to find a suitable one. If, however, your card is of a non-standard size, or you require a specific colour to complement a design that is not available ready made, you could make your own. It is not difficult and the instructions given for this basic envelope can be tailored to fit any size of card.

The measurements are in metric with imperial equivalents in brackets. However, these are not exact conversions as it would unnecessarily complicate things to work in fractions of inches, so I would advise using either one or the other, rather than a combination of the two.

1 Measure the card at its highest and widest points and add 0.5cm (¼in) to each measurement.

2 To work out the size of paper required to make the envelope, you need to add on the following measurements: at least 2.5cm (1in) for each side flap; three quarters of the width of the card plus 1cm (½in) for the base flap; a quarter of the width plus 1cm (½in) for the top flap (see diagram right).

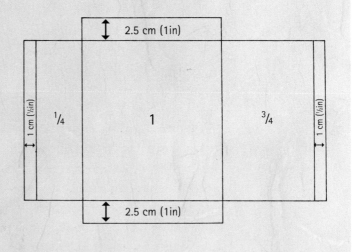

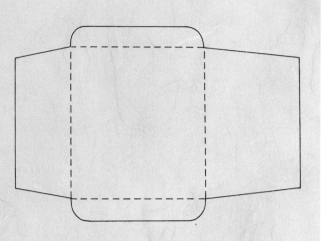

3 Draw the shape shown right onto your chosen paper. Gently taper the top and base flaps and use a coin to draw the curves of the side flaps. Cut out and crease or score along the dotted lines.

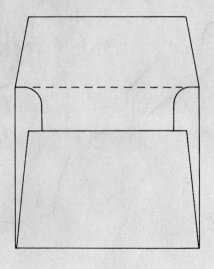

4 To assemble the envelope, turn in the side flaps as shown left. Apply glue to the side edges of the base flap, turn it up and stick it to the side flaps as shown left.

To close the envelope you could use glue, double-sided sticky tape, or for an extra special finish, sealing wax.

If you wish to add a lining to your handmade envelope, cut a piece of tissue or other coloured paper to the size of the envelope minus the base and side flaps, and glue this into position before assembling the envelope.

Whether you choose to make your own envelopes or use ready-made ones, they could both be further enhanced by decorating them. This could range from a few simple stickers to more elaborate designs using giftwrap, fabric, braids, ribbons, glitter glue or sequins. These can be used to decorate corners and borders, both front and back, and could either complement the card inside, or be completely abstract. Whatever design style you choose, be it simple and stylish, or fun and multicoloured, if your envelope is going by

mail, do make sure that any materials used are very firmly attached and as flat as possible, and that you leave enough space for the address and stamps to be seen clearly.

BOXES

Decorated envelopes

The main purpose of boxes is to provide protection for your work, and if you wrap your card in bubble wrap first, to stop it bouncing around inside, any suitably sized, reasonably strong box will do. If you have a look around the house, you will probably find enough to get you started, then save any, as and when you find them. Boxes can also be purchased from greetings card suppliers to fit most of the standard card sizes, they come flat and pre-creased, and take only seconds to construct. If you are planning to sell your cards, these are probably the best option as they will add to the presentation of your work. As for making your own, they are fiddly and time-consuming, and in my opinion your time and energy would probably be better spent creating and producing attractive cards.

CHAPTER 6

Handy
Hints

There are lots of tips throughout the book which relate to specific topics. This chapter concentrates on more general ones, with the aim of making life a bit easier.

WORK AREA

A nice thing about this hobby is that it doesn't require any dedicated workspace. All that is needed is a clean, flat surface. A kitchen or dining room table is ideal, although I would recommend working on some spare sheets of paper or an old magazine. This will not only protect your table, but if you do spill some glue, you can remove the soiled top sheet, leaving a clean base on which to continue working. There is nothing worse than finishing a design only to find it spoiled by spilt glue from a grubby work top.

COMFORT

As with any task where you are seated, it is easier and more enjoyable if you are comfortable, especially if you are going to be there for any length of time. Choose a chair that is the correct height for the table and will encourage good posture as you work. It is also a good idea to take a break now and then, even if you do find it hard to tear yourself away from your latest creation.

LIGHTING

Good light is very important as many of the items you will be working with will be quite small: it will put less strain on your eyes and make colour matching of card and materials much easier. Obviously natural light is best, but if you don't have access to a window or are working in the evening, a desk or table lamp will give off a better light and create fewer shadows than general room lighting.

USING SCISSORS

Always keep the scissors still, turn the paper into the path of the blades as you cut, rather than the other way round, as this tends to be far more accurate and comfortable.

TIME SAVERS

Most of the designs in this book, are already in themselves easy
and quick to complete, but you can speed up this process even
further by gathering together everything you need for each project
before you start. This is also beneficial if you need to stop in the
middle of a construction, as you can then pack away everything
needed to complete the design into a suitable container (a small,
spare shoe box is ideal) which makes it very easy to get out and
pick up where you left off, when you next have time.

If you intend to make more than one card of a chosen design it will
help if you start by making a cardboard template. It is much
quicker and easier to draw round one of these than it is to trace or
draw the design each time. This is especially true when making
invitations, where you may require a large quantity of the same
design. It will also ensure greater consistency from card to card
than other methods.

Off-cuts are useful as
backgrounds and gift
tags. To make a gift tag,
simply punch a hole
and thread through a
length of ribbon.

Another way in which I save a lot of time and effort is by using
off-cuts. These are the punchings from the centre of aperture
greetings card blanks. They are ideal for use as backgrounds and

gift tags as the edges are straight, and the shapes are regular, and this can help to give a more professional finish to your work. They can be purchased individually from some art and craft shops, which is an advantage if you are looking for something specific as it enables you to select the colour, shape and size. However, for more general use, it is much cheaper to buy a mixed bag, usually sold by weight. These are available mail order from suppliers of greetings card blanks.

FINISHING TOUCHES

If you are making a card for a specific occasion, you may wish to add a written greeting on the front. Unless you are very good at calligraphy, I would avoid writing this by hand, as a poorly handwritten message is likely to cheapen the overall effect. Instead, I would recommend choosing a more reliable method, for example,

Fixing an insert sheet

Peel offs, rubber
stamps and stencils
can be used to write
your own greeting

peel offs, rubber stamps, sequins or stencils, which are all available
in a range of greetings. You should also make allowances for your
greeting when planning your design. If you try to add it afterwards
the end result may not be as you'd hoped. Another alternative is to
use pre-printed greetings card blanks, which are available in a
range of greetings to suit most occasions.

Insert sheets are another way of adding a touch of sophistication to
the card as a whole. These are pieces of paper, slightly smaller than
the opened out, finished card, folded in half and glued inside along
the fold. They are often useful on dark coloured cards, where black
or blue ink would not show clearly, and have the advantage with
any card, of allowing you to add as many as you like, perhaps for a
long letter rather than just a short message. If you do not wish to
make your own, these too can be purchased mail order from card
suppliers, either plain, or printed with one of a number of greetings.

CHAPTER 7

Card Making as a Hobby

I know from experience that there are many reasons why people start a hobby and an equal number of reasons why they stop. Across the years I have tried my hand at various hobbies but have given them up because they were either too expensive, took too long to achieve an end product, were difficult to fit in around normal daily life, or simply became too boring doing the same thing all the time. This is not the case with card making: it is cheap, quick, perfectly adaptable, and the design possibilities are endless. It is a very easy hobby to both start, and stick with, and the information given in this chapter should help to smooth this out even further.

GETTING ORGANIZED

When you first start to make and design your own cards and your collection of materials is quite small, it is possible to store them either all together in one box or dotted around the house. However, as your hobby develops and your collection of materials grows, it is much easier to find things if they are stored in a reasonably organized way.

If you want to buy a ready-made storage system, tool boxes with compartments are very good and these can be found in lots of shapes and sizes at any large DIY store. Similarly, art and craft shops sell a variety of custom-made containers which are suitable for keeping small items in, but these can be expensive and it really isn't necessary to buy anything if you don't want to.

There are plenty of other ways to store your materials that won't cost a thing and if you look around the house and in your larder you may find you're spoilt for choice. Small, clear glass jars or pots are excellent as you can see at a glance what they contain, and spice jars or the tiny jam or marmalade pots from hotels and service stations are ideal for storing sequins, stick on eyes, diamantés and beads. Shoe boxes, plastic ice cream tubs and biscuit tins offer protection for items like ribbons, feathers, and silk or dried flowers and can be stacked in order to save space without squashing the contents. Baby change boxes also can be given a new lease of life and it is surprising how much they will hold.

If you are lucky enough to have a shelf or small table where you can leave your materials on permanent display, wicker baskets filled with flowers, ribbons or small pots of sequins look very attractive and these can be bought very cheaply from bric-a-brac and jumble sales.

Whichever storage method you choose, it is important that you can lay your hands on everything you need quickly, so that when inspiration strikes, you can get straight on with putting your ideas together, before the moment is lost.

Recycled tins and jars are useful for storing decorative materials

DESIGNING YOUR OWN CARDS

Following a set of instructions and achieving a pleasing end result is very rewarding, but the real satisfaction comes when you have also designed the card yourself. This may sound a bit daunting at first and whilst it is true that inspiration itself can not be taught, a few pointers in the right direction can help enormously. By making some of the cards in this book you will gain confidence and get a feel for what looks good, and this, along with the ideas given in the next few pages should help to fire your imagination and let you go on to create your own designs.

WHAT TO LOOK OUT FOR

If you begin to look at things with card designing in mind the sources of inspiration are endless. Here are a few pointers to get you going.

Nature alone provides an almost limitless supply of subject material with its trees, plants and flowers, birds and animals, the sky and its ever-changing mood, the sea and seashore, different landscapes, and not forgetting the changes in all of these across the seasons.

Ornamental and decorative things found in and around the home can also help spark off ideas. For example, the inspiration for Merlin's Magic and Fairy and Flowers came from ornaments that had been on my mantelpiece for many years. Similarly, the idea for Pagoda came from an old metal wall sculpture that I picked up at a jumble sale. Look around, you probably have a favourite lamp, vase or garden feature that would make a good subject for a card design.

Groups of colours, shapes, patterns or textures which work well together can provide ideas that you may not have considered before, and you can even theme your cards around the latest fashion colours and styles.

If you are making cards with children in mind, keep an eye on trends in the toy market, if the latest craze is aliens or dinosaurs, this might form the basis for lots of design ideas.

Particular periods in history like medieval, Edwardian, Victorian, Art Deco, or more recently, the seventies with its bold colours and shapes, can start ideas flowing, or think about particular cultures like Indian, African or Chinese. Consider how they live, both now and in the past, how they dress, popular patterns used on fabrics and in the home, how they work and play, or their different customs and beliefs.

With all these possible sources, I would strongly recommend keeping an 'ideas book' to jot things down as they occur to you. It provides one place to keep and organize all of your ideas and will prove invaluable when you need some inspiration for a new card design.

WHERE TO LOOK

The previous section gave a few suggestions on the types of things to look at when searching for design ideas, this section suggests some of the places you might find them.

There are many sources you might find in the home including magazines, catalogues and holiday brochures. Most of these are full of images that will give ideas for colour, shapes and subject material. If you find some that appeal to you, cut them out and use them to start your own picture library. This can be in an old shoe box or even a carrier bag, either way, it is great fun to sort through this now and again, especially when you have forgotten what is in there. Other items to save for your library could include postcards, old greetings cards and bits of wallpaper or fabric.

Children's books often have beautiful and inspiring illustrations, and painting and colouring books are full of fairly simple line drawings that can be modified.

Look through your photo album: an old holiday or party snap can often spark off an idea, you could even use the photo itself and incorporate it into a design for a really personal touch.

A little further afield, you will find what I think is the best source for inspiration there is, the local library. With thousands of books, covering almost as many topics, it is a designer's paradise, and whatever your interests, an hour spent here with your 'ideas book' for notes should provide no end of material.

Museums, exhibitions and even shop window displays can provide many new ideas, so if you are off out for the day, remember to take your note book with you. If you are visiting an event or show, save the programme or brochure, as these often have high gloss, brightly coloured photos, of fabulous costumes or scene sets, or interesting and unusual objects, and may prove useful later.

Materials themselves can also be used to inspire, and once you have gathered together a nice collection, sort through them once in a while. Many of my designs started life based on the things I already had.

Wherever you take your ideas from, it is important that you do not copy other people's work, including photographs, as they may be subject to copyright, but you may of course use anything you see to spark off ideas for creations of your own.

My final piece of advice when designing your own cards is don't be afraid to experiment. Even if it doesn't turn out quite as you'd hoped, it is rare that you can't save a design by adding a few sequins, bows or similar. If the worst happens and it still isn't right, put that one down to experience, it won't have cost much, just a little time, and with each mistake you will learn and improve.

GIFT CARDS

A very nice touch when making your own cards is to incorporate a gift into the design. With Glamour Girl I have shown two ways to use this card, with the gift being either earrings or a necklace. There are many other small gifts that could be worked into a design including hair accessories, cuff links, tie pins, fishing floats or flies, or small toys or badges for children. This is an unusual and original way of giving both a card and a gift.

GIFT TAGS

If you are giving a separate card and gift, complement your card by making a matching gift tag. Try picking out a small detail from your design or maybe just the colours. To show your tag at its best, don't use highly patterned wrapping paper, single colour or plain brown, tied with raffia or ribbon will look very stylish and provide the perfect backdrop. Gift tag blanks can be purchased in a range of styles and finishes, but if you wish to make your own, they are made in exactly the same way as full-sized cards, only much smaller.

BOOKMARKS

These too can be given as a small, but thoughtful gift. Bear in mind though when designing them, that they need to be fairly flat. Bookmark blanks are available from art and craft shops and card suppliers.

A selection of bookmarks and gift tags

CARDS FOR SALE

Once you become hooked on this pastime, you will probably find yourself producing more cards than you can use. If this is the case, you could start off by selling any surplus to friends and family, who are usually very eager to take them off your hands. As your confidence grows and your stocks increase even further, you might like to consider selling your cards at craft fairs, or maybe even approach your local craft shop. Craft fairs are a great day out, you can meet lots of interesting people and pick up plenty of tips and ideas.

Handmade cards are very popular and as lots of people send lots of cards every year, there is always a potential market for your handiwork, but do make sure that any you sell are your own designs.

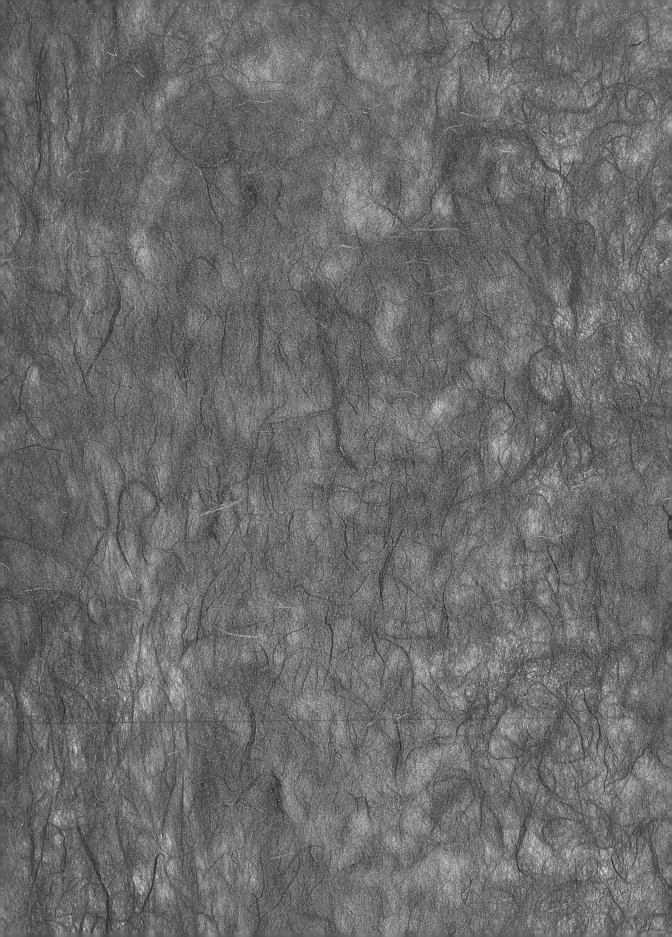

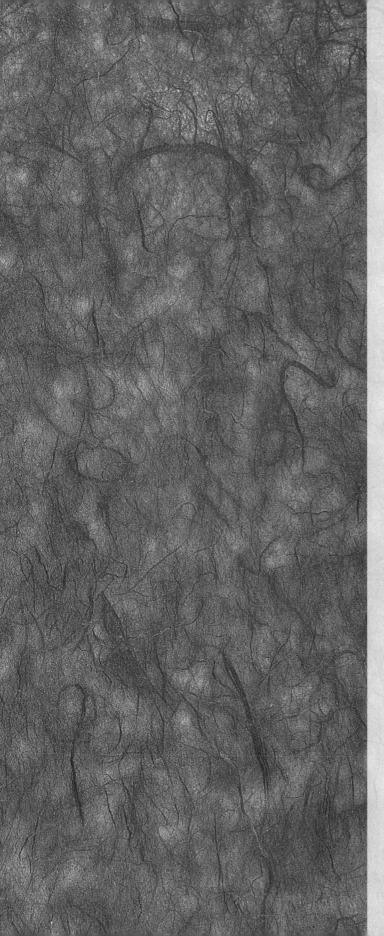

CHAPTER 8

The Cards

THE CARDS

The cards on the following pages have been chosen to cover a wide range of styles and occasions, and whether you are a beginner or an old hand, there should be something to suit all tastes. They have been put in the order of the time needed to make them, starting with those taking less than 15 minutes and ending with those which may take an hour or so. The times given are only estimates, and are based on the assumption that you have everything you need to hand including the card mount. However, the most important thing is to work at your own pace, and not to get discouraged if it takes slightly longer to complete a card than I have suggested. This is just a guide to show what might be achieved if you only have a little time to spare.

Most of the designs are suitable for many different occasions just as they are, but you could make some of them even more versatile by adding a few hearts for a valentine card, changing the colours for an Easter or sympathy card or adding numbers for special birthdays. For this reason I have not specified occasions for any of the projects, other than those designed for a specific purpose, but have just offered suggestions for a few of the many different ways they might be used.

The colours suggested are just a personal preference, and you may like to substitute your own, as you can completely change the feel of a card simply by changing the colours. For example, Midnight Moggy would be given a totally different look if worked up in daytime colours with a sun instead of the moon.

Many of these are also ideal for framing, so you may like to give a suitable frame as an accompanying gift, or frame it before sending.

However you interpret these designs, I feel sure they will give both you, and those who receive them, a great deal of pleasure.

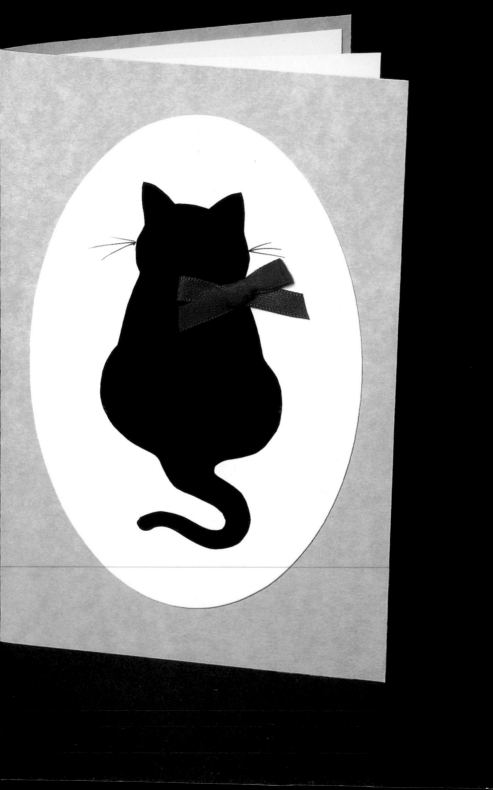

FASHIONABLE FELINE

This silhouette is both striking and sophisticated yet very easy to make. It could be given to cat lovers on almost any occasion and would make an ideal 'good luck' card for a new job, driving test or any other event when you would like to send someone your best wishes. For the background I have used an oval offcut of card, but it would work equally well with a rectangle or, on a pale coloured card, without one at all.

1 Trace the cat template and cut one from black paper.

2 Glue the oval offcut onto the front of the card.

3 Glue cat and bow onto the offcut.

Single-fold card
114 x 178mm
(4½ x 7in)

Oval offcut
94 x 145mm
(3¾ x 5¾in)

Small quantity of
black paper

7mm (¼in)
wide ribbon bow

Black pen

Less than 15 minutes

4 Draw whiskers with a black pen.

CELESTIAL

This card is the simplest and quickest of them all yet loses nothing in the way of style or effect. It requires no tracing and uses just a small piece of mulberry paper and a few sequins. This card could be used as an ideal way of staying in touch as well as a whole host of other occasions. This basic design is very adaptable and by changing the colour of the paper and using different sequins you could even turn it into a Christmas or Halloween card.

1. Glue the mulberry paper onto the front of the card by adding small dots of glue to correspond with the positions of the sequins. This will avoid any risk of the glue showing from the front.

2. Glue the sequins in place.

Single-fold card
104 x 152mm
(4 x 6in)

Small square of
mulberry paper
(see Chapter 5 for
how to tear this)

A few celestial
sequins

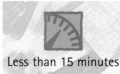

Less than 15 minutes

DOLPHIN DISPLAY

This is another card that could be used for almost any occasion and dolphins are a popular subject with both young and old, male and female. For this design, I have used an aperture card, and graduated paper, but it could be worked on a single-fold card or using a plain background. You could even use a suitable picture of the sea cut from a magazine behind the dolphin.

1 Trace the dolphin template and cut one from black paper.

2 Glue the background paper behind the aperture, then glue the front flap of the card to the inside to cover the background paper.

3 Cut the foam pad into four or five smaller pieces and use these to stick the dolphin onto the background paper, within the aperture, as shown.

Double-fold oval aperture card with gold borderline: card size 104 x 152mm (4 x 6in), aperture 76 x 114mm (3 x 4½in)

Graduated paper for background

Small quantity of black paper

Moon and stars sequins

1 double-sided foam pad

Less than 15 minutes

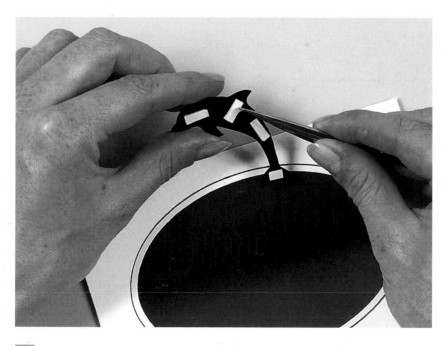

4 Glue on the sequins.

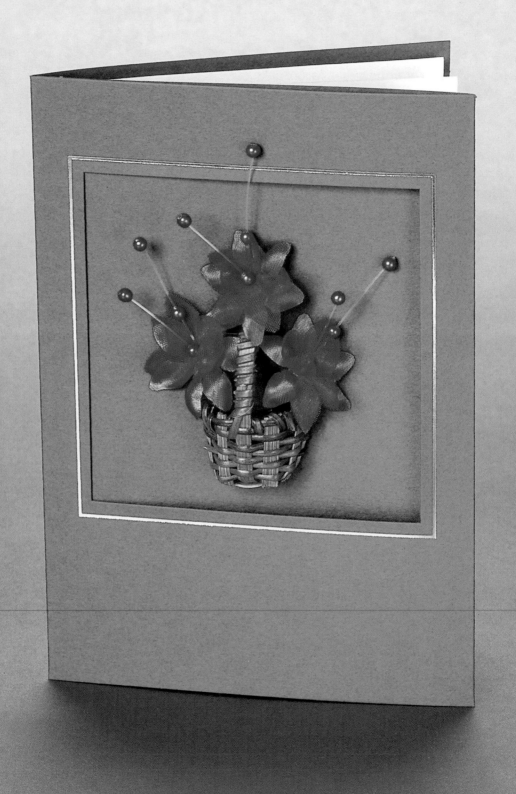

BEAD FLOWER BASKET

It is always nice to receive a basket of flowers and this would be no exception. It could be given for birthdays, Mother's Day or anniversaries, and would be a lovely way to cheer up someone who is unwell. If you use springtime colours, it could also be given as an Easter card. It works equally well on a single-fold card, with or without a background, and you could substitute the flowers for those of your choice.

1 Cut the foam pads into smaller pieces and use to secure the front flap of the card to the inside, behind the aperture, to give extra depth.

2 Using sharp scissors, cut the basket in half.

Double-fold square aperture card with gold borderline: card size 104 x 152mm (4 x 6in), aperture 79 x 82mm (3 x 3¼in)

Miniature wicker basket

3 silk flowers

Double-sided foam pads

Less than 15 minutes

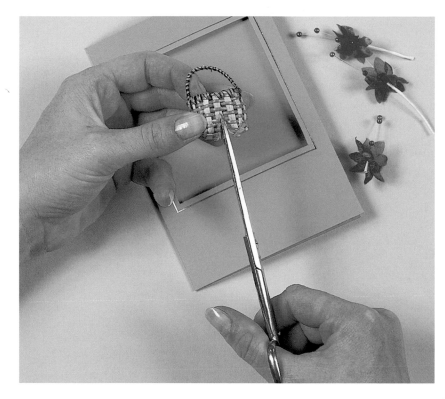

3 Apply glue to the cut edges of the basket and stick into position within the aperture as shown.

4 Trim the flower stems and stick onto the card.

CHARLESTON CHIC

This design conjures up images of a bygone era and is equally at home in a frame. It could not only be given for many of the traditional occasions like birthdays or Mother's Day, but it would also make an unusual and original party invitation or 'good luck with the show' card. I have used pre-strung sequins but you could use individual ones. Although this card uses only the tip of the feather the remainder can be saved for use in another design.

1 Trace the template for the head and cut one from black paper.

2 Glue the offcut onto the card, and the head onto the offcut.

3 Cut the sequin string to the required length and glue into position for the headband as shown.

4 Cut the tip from the feather and glue into place.

Single-fold deckle-edge card 114 x 178mm (4½ x 7in)

Oval offcut 94 x 145mm (3¾ x 5¾in)

Small quantity of black paper

Short length of pre-strung sequins

1 small feather

Less than 15 minutes

WOODLAND

The universal appeal of this woodland scene makes it suitable for both males and females on almost any occasion. It works equally well with lighter coloured card and brighter flowers, and you may also like to add a contrasting backing sheet behind the aperture before fixing the items. This design would also lend itself to being mounted in a suitable box frame and would make a nice gift for a new home.

1 Cut the foam pads into smaller pieces and use to secure the front flap of the card to the inside, behind the aperture, to give extra depth.

2 Carefully cut the mushrooms in half lengthways.

3 Glue the mushroom halves onto the card within the aperture as shown.

4 Glue the moss and dried flowers around the base of the mushrooms.

Double-fold oval aperture card with gold borderline: card size 104 x 152mm (4 x 6in), aperture 76 x 114mm (3 x 4½in)

2 artificial mushrooms (1 large, 1 small)

Small quantity of dried flowers and moss

Double-sided foam pads

Less than 30 minutes

PAGODA

This design is eye-catching, but simple, and could be just the thing to send to someone who is normally quite difficult to buy for. For the tree I have used a piece of pressed conifer sprayed with gold paint, but you could use artificial or dried foliage and either spray it, or leave it natural. If you want to press your own, place it between the pages of a telephone directory, well weighted down, or a flower press, for a few weeks until it has dried out.

1. Trace templates for the pagoda pieces and cut from black paper. Trace the template for the base and cut two from gold card.

2. Glue the white card within the borderline.

3. Glue the risers and the bases onto the card.

4. Using the gold pen, draw 'tiles' onto the roof pieces. They look better if the vertical lines are drawn straight down through all the pieces, rather than randomly spaced.

5. Cut the foam pads into smaller pieces and use these to stick the roof pieces on top of the risers as shown.

6. Glue the foliage in place.

Single-fold card
150 x 203mm
(6 x 8in)
with oblong gold
borderline

White card approx.
95 x 145mm
(3¾ x 5¾in)

Small quantity of
black paper and gold
card

Piece of foliage

Gold pen

Double-sided foam
pads

Less than 30 minutes

MIDNIGHT MOGGY

This design is ideal for cat lovers of all ages and could be given for all manner of reasons. It would be a very nice way to let someone know you are thinking of them or perhaps as an invitation to a 'night on the town'. For the sky I have used handmade paper with tiny bits of foil embedded into it to give a starry look, but this is not essential as a similar effect can be achieved by using a plain backing (or none at all if using a dark blue card) and gluing on star-shaped sequins.

1. Glue the handmade paper centrally on to the back of the front flap, so that it will show through the aperture when the card is closed.

2. Trace templates for the house and the cat on the wall and cut one of each from black paper.

3. Add moonlight detail to the cat and the wall with gold pen.

4. Glue the house on to the handmade paper as shown. Glue the cat on the wall to the inside of the aperture as shown.

5. Cut the foam pads into smaller pieces and use these to secure the front flap of the card to the inside, behind the aperture, to give extra depth.

6. Cut a moon from the gold card or foil using a coin as a template, and glue in place.

Double-fold oblong aperture card with gold borderline: card size 150 x 203mm (6 x 8in), aperture 94 x 145mm (3¾ x 5¾in)

Piece of handmade paper approx. 135 x 190mm (5¼ x 7½in)

Small quantity of black paper and gold card or foil

Gold pen

Double-sided foam pads

Less than 30 minutes

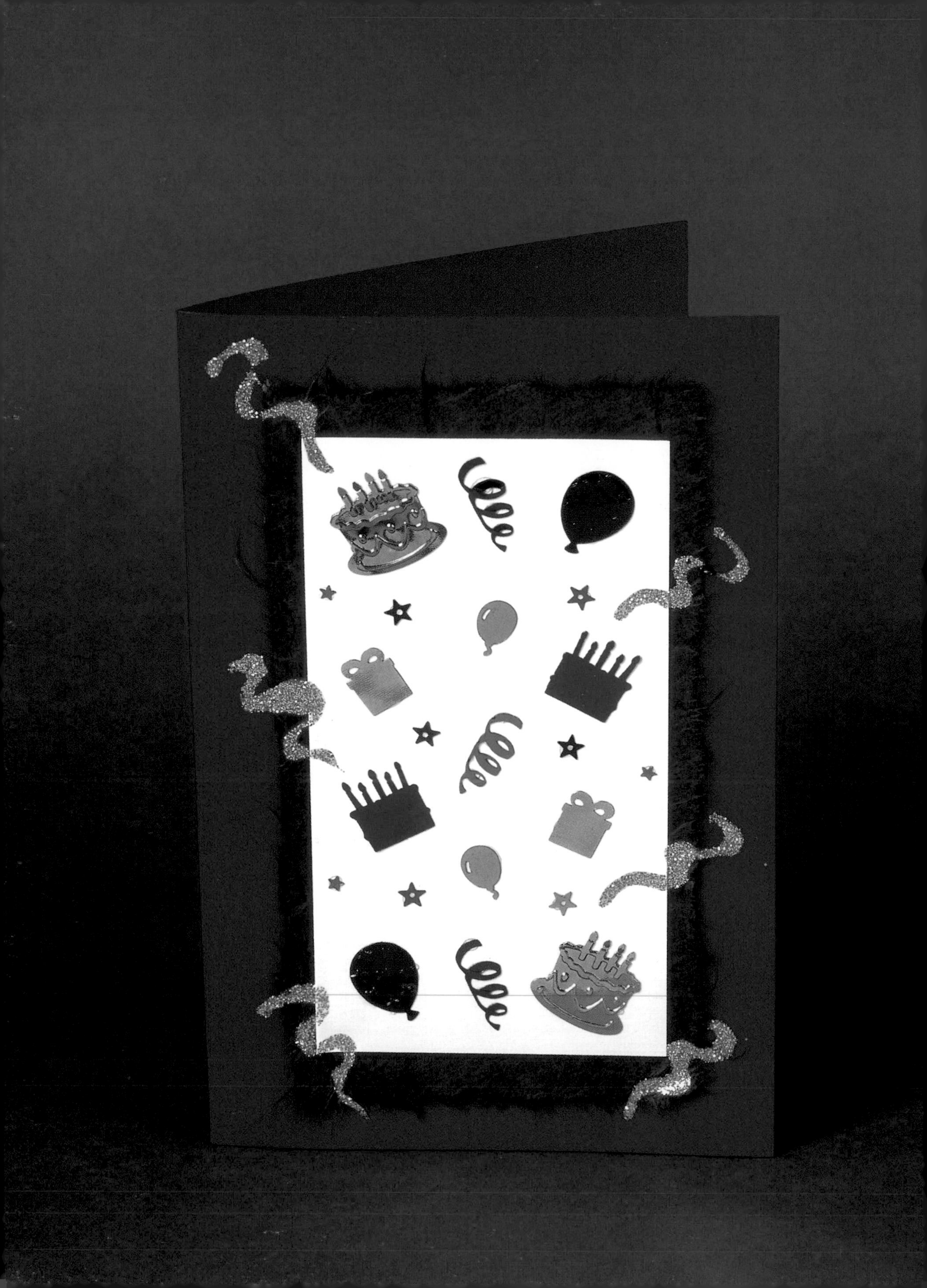

BIRTHDAY BONANZA

This is an extremely useful and versatile design as it could be given to almost anyone, and by changing the sequins, for nearly any occasion. Sequin confetti is available in a huge range and by using this basic design as the starting point, you can create a variety of cards, including new baby, anniversary, wedding and Christmas.

1. Glue the mulberry paper onto the front of the card, then glue the white card onto the mulberry paper.

2. Arrange the sequins how you wish, then glue them onto the card.

3. Draw squiggles around the edges using glitter glue.

Single-fold card
114 x 178mm
(4½ x 7in)

Piece of mulberry
paper approx.
90 x 150mm
(3½ x 6in)
(see Chapter 5 for
how best to tear this)

White card approx.
70 x 130mm
(2¾ x 5in)

Selection of sequins

Glitter glue

Less than 30 minutes

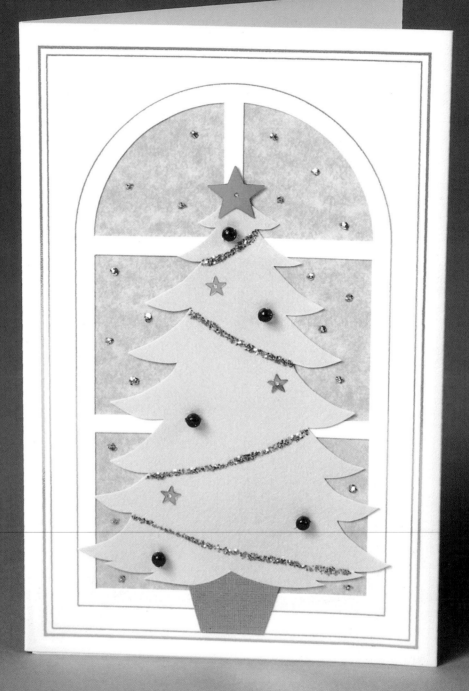

WHITE CHRISTMAS

This is a very sophisticated Christmas card and would be ideal to send to someone special. I have used grey parchment-effect paper for the background, and card with a pearl finish for the tree, but you could replace these with plain coloured card if you wish. For a quicker but equally effective alternative, you could take the tree and pot from this design and put it on a plain, single-fold card. The time saved could add up significantly if you have a lot of cards to send.

1. Trace templates for the tree and pot and cut one of each from the appropriate card.

2. Glue the background paper behind the aperture, then glue the front flap of the card to the inside, to cover the background paper.

3. Glue the tree and pot onto the front of the card, then glue the stars and beads onto the tree.

Double-fold card with window aperture and gold borderlines: card size 114 x 178mm (4½ x 7in), aperture 73 x 137mm (3 x 5½in)

Grey parchment-effect paper for background

Small quantity of pearl-finished card for tree, and gold card for pot

1 large and 3 small, star-shaped sequins

5 small red beads

Gold and silver glitter glue

Less than 30 minutes

4. Draw 'tinsel' around the tree using gold glitter glue, and 'snow' onto the background, using silver glitter glue.

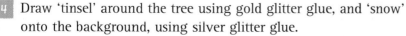

MASQUERADE

It is often difficult to choose a card for a teenager, and this fun and lively design could be one solution. It would make an acceptable birthday card for many age groups and would also make a stylish invitation to a 'not to be missed' party. I have used a piece of feather and sequins to decorate this one, but the basic mask shape could be used for all manner of elaborate creations. The small gold mask, which was originally intended for use with modelling clay, is optional, and if you were to use small hearts instead of stars, this would make a very original valentine card.

1 Trace the template for the mask and cut one from black paper.

2 Glue the mulberry paper onto the front of the card, then glue on the mask.

3 Glue on sequins, feather and small gold mask.

4 Add glitter glue detail around the eyes.

Single-fold card
114 x 178mm
(4½ x 7in)

Piece of mulberry
paper approx.
80 x 145mm
(3¼ x 5¾in)
(see Chapter 5 for
how best to tear this)

Small quantity of
black paper

Piece of feather

Star and snowflake
sequins

Small gold mask

Gold glitter glue

Less than 30 minutes

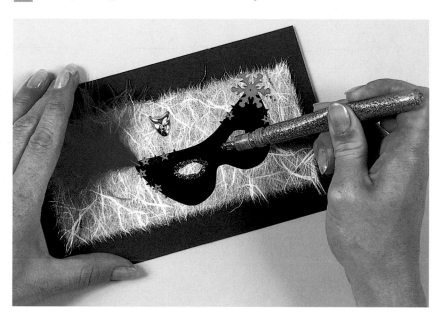

UNDER THE SEA

This card is simple to make but very effective. It could be given for almost any occasion, and would make an unusual 'New Home' card. It is also ideal for framing and might be sent either with a suitable box frame for mounting later or pre-mounted as a complete gift. For this design I have used pressed leaves and grasses, but artificial ones would look just as nice. If you want to press your own, place them between the pages of a telephone directory, well weighted down, or a flower press, for a few weeks until they are dry and papery to the touch.

1. Arrange your chosen selection of leaves, grasses, shells and stones on the front of the card until you are happy with them. Place them in a straight line near to the base of the card and group them with gaps in between as this tends to look more realistic than a solid line.

2. Glue your final arrangement in place.

Single-fold card
150 x 203mm
(6 x 8in)

A few pressed leaves and grasses (different shapes and colours will make it more interesting)

A few small seashells and stones or gravel

Paper sea horse

Less than 30 minutes

3. Glue the sea horse onto the card.

FAIRY AND FLOWERS

Whether 5 or 55, this dainty little fairy has proved appealing to all ages, and can be used to send good wishes for all sorts of reasons like birthdays, Mother's Day, 'get well' or 'thank you'. The bouquet of flowers has been cut from a length of braid, but as an alternative, use dried or silk flowers. The wings are worked in glitter glue and because a delicate appearance is important, I would recommend practising on scraps first, until you are confident about achieving the correct pressure.

1 Trace template for the fairy and cut one from black paper.

2 Glue the offcut onto the front of the card, then glue the fairy onto the offcut.

3 Glue the bow and the flower in place.

4 Trace template for the wings.

5 Turn the tracing paper over and lay it directly onto the card in the position shown in the picture. Gently redraw the lines to leave a faint impression.

Single-fold
deckle-edge card
114 x 178mm
(4½ x 7in)

Oval offcut
94 x 145mm
(3¾ x 5¾in)

Small quantity of
black paper

7mm (¼in) wide
ribbon bow

Flower

Silver glitter glue

Less than 30 minutes

6 Go over these lines with silver glitter glue to finish the wings.

unicorn

This card would make a lovely general purpose card for a wide age range, and would be particularly suitable to send to anyone with a New Age outlook or just a good old-fashioned romantic. The fantasy aspect of this design is enhanced by the pearl-finished card and glittery handmade paper, but if you do not have these, you could use plain coloured card or paper and add detail to the background with sequins or glitter glue. For a traditional horse, leave off the horn and change the colour scheme, you could also replace the bow with a gold horseshoe like those used for cake decorating.

1 Trace template for the unicorn and cut one from pearl-finished card.

2 Cut a long, thin triangle from silver card for the horn and glue onto the unicorn as shown.

3 Cutting close to the quill, remove the down from one side of the feather, then glue it along the neck of the Unicorn.

4 Glue the unicorn behind the aperture, then glue the background paper behind this.

5 Glue the front flap of the card closed.

6 Glue on the silver bow.

Double-fold square aperture card: card size 150 x 203mm (6 x 8in), aperture 101 x 101mm (4 x 4in)

Small quantity of handmade paper for the background

Small quantity of pearl-finished card and silver card

1 small feather

Silver bow

Less than 30 minutes

FLYING SOUTH

This is a very peaceful scene and seems to particularly appeal to outdoor types like anglers, ramblers and bird watchers, and would make a lovely birthday or Father's Day card. It can also be worked in bright colours to give a completely different feel to it, which extends its appeal to many others.

1 Trace templates for the duck and the water and cut from the appropriate paper.

2 Cut two pieces from the chenille stem for the bulrushes.

3 Glue the ducks, water and bulrushes onto the front of the card as shown.

Single-fold card
104 x 152mm
(4 x 6in)

Small quantity of paper in black, olive and dark green

Brown chenille stem

Gold pen

Less than 30 minutes

4 Using the gold pen, draw the bulrush stems and leaves, and water detail.

CHRISTMAS CANDLE

This arrangement is put together in much the same way as a real one, with the foliage either inserted, or stuck on, to a small piece of dry floral foam. You may like to try using more traditional Christmas leaves like holly, which could either be sprayed, or left green. I have used an aperture card with a gold borderline to 'frame' the display, but a similar effect could be achieved by mounting it on an oval offcut and then onto a single-fold card. I would recommend using a glue gun for this project, due to the tightly packed and rather fiddly nature of the pieces.

1 Glue the front flap of the card behind the aperture to close.

2 Glue the floral foam within the aperture as shown.

3 Put the candle into the holder, then insert the holder into the floral foam.

4 Add foliage around the candle by inserting it in the floral foam.

5 Glue moss to any exposed areas of the floral foam.

6 Glue the flowers around the base.

Double-fold oval aperture card with gold borderline: card size 104 x 152mm (4 x 6in), aperture 76 x 114mm (3 x 4½in)

Very small piece of dry floral foam (commonly known as Oasis®)

Small quantity of dried flowers and moss

3 small silk flowers

1 birthday cake candle and holder

Less than 30 minutes

Safety note - this card uses a small birthday cake candle for its centre piece, but this is obviously for decoration only and must never be lit.

MERLIN'S MAGIC

This design works equally as well as a birthday or Father's Day card as it does for Halloween, and you could even turn it into a valentine's card by adding a suitable 'under my spell' verse inside. The mulberry paper is used to give the effect of a flash of light, but this is not essential as Merlin also looks very good on his own, on a plain white card.

1 Trace template for the wizard and cut one from black paper.

2 Lay the wizard onto the mulberry paper. Leaving a border and using the basic shape as a guide, draw a line around him with a wet paintbrush. Ease the paper apart along this line.

Single-fold card
114 x 178mm
(4½ x 7in)

Small piece of black paper

Piece of mulberry paper

Stars and moons sequins

Silver glitter glue

Less than 30 minutes

3 Glue the mulberry paper onto the front of the card, and the wizard shape onto this.

4 Glue the stars and moons sequins onto the cloak, and add a few more rising from the bottle.

5 Add glitter glue dots between the sequins as shown.

CHAMPAGNE

This card is perfect for any celebration and can easily be modified to suit specific events. If you add another glass it makes a lovely anniversary card and by changing the colour of the bow, it can be tailored for silver, ruby or golden wedding anniversaries. You could replace the glitter glue fountain and stars for a shower of confetti for a wedding card, or add foil numbers for a special birthday. I was lucky enough to find this champagne bottle on a sheet of wrapping paper but it would work just as well if cut from black or dark green paper, and the detail added with a gold pen. A template for this can be found at the back of the book.

1. Trace template for the champagne bottle and cut one from black or dark green paper. Add detail with gold pen and glue onto the card as shown.

2. Using a pencil, very lightly draw one or two glasses onto the card (use a coin to draw the bowl of the glass).

3. Glue a few sequins and the bow onto the card.

4. Use the glitter glues to make the fountain.

5. Use silver and gold glues on your glass to outline, and to fill it.

Single-fold card with embossed border
114 x 178mm
(4½ x 7in)

Small quantity of black or dark green paper

7mm (¼in) wide ribbon bow

A few star sequins

Gold pen

Glitter glue in several colours including gold and silver

Less than 30 minutes

ROSES, HEARTS AND LACE

This design has quite a romantic feel and would make a lovely valentine, Mother's Day or birthday card, for someone special. The handmade mulberry paper works well with the delicate lace edging but other papers can be used to give a different effect. This design also works equally well with other aperture shapes.

1 Turn the card face down and glue the lace around the aperture on the inside of the card.

2 Cut a piece of mulberry paper large enough to cover the aperture and glue this to the inside front flap of the card.

3 Cut the foam pads into smaller pieces and use to secure the front flap of the card to the inside, behind the aperture, to give extra depth.

4 Trace template for the hand and cut one from black paper.

5 Glue the hand onto the mulberry paper within the aperture as shown.

6 Glue on diamantés and rosebud, then add bow and sequins to the front face of the card.

Double-fold card with heart-shaped aperture: card size 150 x 203mm (6 x 8in), aperture 101 x 97mm (4 x 3¾in)

Small quantity of black paper

Small quantity of mulberry paper

0.5m (20in) ruffled lace

7mm (¼in) wide ribbon bow

1 large ribbon rosebud

1 large and 2 small heart sequins

Small diamantés

Double-sided foam pads

Less than 30 minutes

KIDS' CLOWN

This colourful clown makes a great card for children of all ages and it would also make a very memorable party invitation. I have given him multicoloured hair, but you could use a single colour or maybe even try a piece of fur fabric for a different effect. For his hat I have used gold card with glitter glue dots, which look very effective but you could use sequins instead.

1 Trace template for the hat and cut one from gold card.

2 Cut wool into short lengths. Take several of these strands and bind together tightly at one end with tape. Trim bound end and glue to one side on the back of the hat. Repeat this for the other side of the hair.

Single-fold deckle-edge card 114 x 178mm (4½ x 7in)

Oval offcut 94 x 145mm (3¾ x 5¾in)

Small quantity of gold card

Small pompom

Scraps of wool and some sticky tape

Pair of 7mm (¼in) stick-on eyes

1 large red bead

1 red star sequin

3mm wide black ribbon bow

Glitter glue

Pencil and black pen

Less than 30 minutes

3 Glue the offcut onto the front of the card.

4 Glue the hat onto the card as shown, and glue the pompom onto the top of the hat.

5 Glue on eyes, nose, mouth and bow.

6 Use pencil to draw eyebrows and black pen for eyelashes. Add glitter glue dots to the hat.

PEN AND POT

This design is not only suitable for birthdays and many other traditional occasions, but could also be used to say 'please write' or 'good luck' with your studies or exams. You may even like to write your own short message on the slip of paper inside the envelope.

1. Trace template for the ink pot and cut one from black paper.

2. Make a small envelope by cutting a square of coloured paper 50 x 50mm (2 x 2in). With wrong side up, turn the paper so that one of the points is at the top. Fold in the side flaps to meet in the middle. Fold up bottom flap and glue being careful not to stick the back and front of the envelope together or you will not be able to insert your 'letter'.

Single-fold deckle-edge card 114 x 178mm (4½ x 7in)

Small quantity of paper in black, white and colour to match feather

1 small feather

Less than 30 minutes

3. Cut a small piece of white paper to fit inside the envelope.

4. Glue the ink pot, feather and envelope in place as shown.

GLAMOUR GIRL

This sophisticated lady makes the perfect gift card to send to someone special. Just add a pair of earrings, which can be anything from homemade to diamonds, to make an original and thoughtful present. This design is also suitable for use with a small, chain necklace (see inset photo opposite). To do this, use a scalpel or craft knife, carefully cut a slit where the neck joins the shoulders, and gently feed the chain through until it is the required length. Put the excess ends of the chain into a small plastic bag and tape to the inside of your card.

1. Trace the head and the hat templates and cut head from black paper and hat from grey. Glue onto the front of the card as shown.

2. Cut a short length of black ribbon to fit across the hat and glue into place. Glue ribbon rosebud onto the hat.

3. Open card out flat so as not to pierce through the back, and with a pin make a small hole through each earlobe to allow earrings to be fitted.

Single-fold card
104 x 152mm
(4 x 6in)

Small quantity of
paper in black and
grey

Short length of black
3mm (⅛in)
wide ribbon

1 small ribbon
rosebud

Pair of earrings

Less than 30 minutes

4. Attach earrings.

97

IT'S A BOY!

This is a lovely card to send to celebrate the birth of a new baby and can obviously be made up in pink for a girl, or red to celebrate a first Christmas.

1 Trace template for the bootees and cut one from spare card.

2 Fold fabric so that right sides are together. Using the card template you have just made, draw round it twice onto the fabric to give two bootees and cut out.

3 Leaving the top open, run a line of glue around the edge, on the right side of the fabric, on one piece of each bootee. Lay the other corresponding pieces right side down onto the glued pieces. Leave to dry.

4 Glue the blue card onto the front of your card and the white handmade paper onto this.

5 Glue a teddy sequin on each corner.

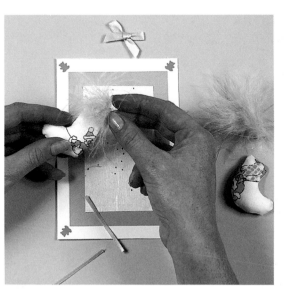

6 When dry, turn the bootees right side out and lightly stuff. Fold in top edges and glue to close.

7 Glue a small piece of marabou across the top of each bootee.

8 Cut two pieces of ribbon to the required length and glue one piece onto each bootee. Glue the other ends together onto the card near the top. Glue the ribbon bow over these ends.

Single-fold card
104 x 152mm
(4 x 6in)

Blue card approx.
85 x 130mm
(3¼ x 5in)

White handmade
paper approx.
60 x 105mm
(2¼ x 4in)

Small quantity of
fabric and a little
stuffing.

Short length of
marabou edging

Short length of pale
blue 3mm (⅛in)
wide ribbon

7mm (¼in) wide pale
blue ribbon bow

4 blue teddy bear
sequins

Small piece of spare
card

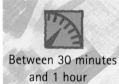

Between 30 minutes
and 1 hour

SUITED AND BOOTED

This card is not only appropriate for birthdays and Father's Day, but could also be used to say 'sorry you're leaving' or 'good luck in your new job'. If the person you are giving this to has a particular taste in shirts or ties, you could try to accommodate this in your card.

1 Make a tie using the ribbon. Knot the tie in the same way as a real one, using a pencil as a 'neck'. When you have made your tie, slip it off the pencil and cut the loop to give two ends. Place it centrally at the top edge of the aperture and glue the ends behind the aperture so that the knot shows from the front.

Double-fold square aperture card with gold borderline: card size 104 x 152mm (4 x 6in), aperture 79 x 82mm (3 x 3¼in)

Piece of card for shirt and pocket

Small quantity of white card for collars

Piece of ribbon for tie and hankie

Black pen

2 Cut two collar shapes from white card and glue them behind the aperture, on either side of the tie.

3 Turn the card face down and run a line of glue around the aperture on the inside. Stick down your chosen shirt material, then glue the front flap of the card to the inside to close.

4 Cut a pocket shape from card and a hankie from ribbon. Glue the hankie behind the pocket and then stick the pocket onto the shirt. With a black pen draw tiny 'stitches' around the pocket edges.

Between 30 minutes and 1 hour

ROOM WITH A VIEW

The 'view' I have chosen is one of sky and trees, but the possibilities are endless. Use one of your own photographs, perhaps of a garden, or maybe a picture from a magazine. It would make it even more special if you could find something relevant or personal to the receiver.

1. Trace template for the door and cut two from veneer or card, reversing the template for one of the doors to get a matching pair. Trace template for the balustrade and cut one from light grey card.

2. Place the card mount face down and glue doors onto each side of aperture, so that they will be visible from the front of the card as shown.

3. Separately glue the balustrade to the floor, then glue these onto the aperture behind the doors.

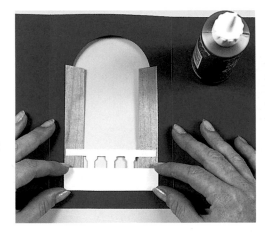

4. With the gold pen, draw a window frame onto the front of the acetate. Glue this behind the aperture, above the doors.

5. Glue your chosen 'view' onto the inside front flap of the card so that it will show through the aperture when closed. If you are using pressed foliage, glue these into place.

6. Cut foam pads into smaller pieces and use them to secure the front flap of the card to the inside, behind the aperture, to give extra depth.

7. Glue gold beads onto the doors.

Double-fold round arch aperture card with gold borderlines: card size 114 x 178mm (4½ x 7in), aperture 73 x 137mm (3 x 5¼in)

Photograph or picture

Small quantity of wood veneer (or brown card)

Small quantity of light grey card (balustrade)

Pale marbled card 85 x 20mm (3¼ x ¾in) (floor)

Clear acetate 85 x 35mm (3¼ x 1¼in) (window)

2 small gold beads and gold pen

2 pieces of pressed foliage

Double-sided foam pads

Between 30 minutes and 1 hour

GOLDEN WEDDING

A golden wedding anniversary is something to celebrate and deserves a special card. This one fits the bill and is easier to make than it looks. If using foiled paper for the numbers as I have, I would recommend using spray adhesive to get an even coverage, and if you have one, a glue gun for the flowers, for a fast hold. This design could also be used for a 50th birthday, and the basic idea could be adapted to make a card for any age. I have also shown examples of both silver and ruby wedding cards and templates for these too can be found at the back of the book.

1. Trace templates for the numbers and cut from gold foil. Glue these onto the front of the card as shown.

2. Glue a small arrangement of dried flowers near to the base of each number.

Single-fold card
114 x 178mm
(4½ x 7in)

Small quantity of
gold foil paper

Small quantity of
dried flowers

Between 30 minutes
and 1 hour

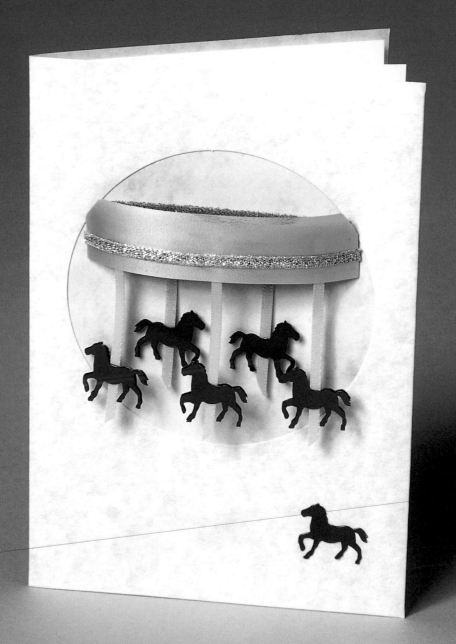

MERRY-GO-ROUND

The pastel colours of this card make it ideal for baby events such as birth, christening or first birthday, but in bolder colours it would suit other age groups as well. I have used an aperture card but it could also be worked on a single-fold card, with or without a background.

1 Glue background card behind the aperture, then glue the front flap of the card closed.

2 Trace template for the merry-go-round top and cut one from spare card. Use this to draw round onto foam and cut out.

3 Cut five pieces of 3mm (⅛in) wide ribbon. These can be any length that suits but make sure you have three slightly longer pieces of equal length for the front and two shorter ones of equal length for the back.

4 Sandwich each piece of ribbon between two sequin horses, near to one end, and glue in place.

5 Glue the three longer pieces of ribbon, evenly spaced, onto the front, curved edge of the foam. Then glue the two shorter ones to the back, straight edge of the foam.

6 Glue the wider ribbon along the front edge to hide the foam.

7 Run a line of glue along the back edge of the foam and stick onto the card.

8 Glue the last sequin horse onto the bottom corner of the card.

Double-fold circle aperture card:

card size
104 x 152mm
(4 x 6in),
aperture
83mm (3¼in)
diameter

A small quantity of card for background

Small piece of foam approx. 15mm (½in) deep

Short length of approx. 20mm (¾in) wide ribbon

Short length of 3mm (⅛in) wide ribbon for 'poles'

11 sequin horses

Spare piece of card

Between 30 minutes and 1 hour

THE BIG DAY

This elegant couple make an attractive and unusual card to give to the bride and groom on their wedding day. Ribbon rosebuds and bows are available in a large range of colours, so if you know in advance the colour of the bride's bouquet, it would be rather nice to use the same on your card.

1. Trace template for the head and cut two from black paper.

2. Trace templates for the hats and cut one of each from grey paper.

3. Trace template for the shirt front and cut one from pearl or white card.

4. Glue both heads into place on the front of the card as shown.

5. Glue a piece of black ribbon across each hat and then glue hats into place.

Single-fold card
104 x 152 mm
(4 x 6in)

Small quantity
of paper in black
and grey

Very small piece
of pearl or plain
white card

Short length of black
3mm (⅛in)
wide ribbon

1 ribbon rosebud and
1 matching 7mm
(¼in) wide ribbon bow

2 small diamantés

Between 30 minutes
and 1 hour

6. Glue rosebud, earrings and shirt front into place.

7. Take the ribbon bow and fold the ends behind the loops and glue into place to give a bow tie shape. Glue this onto the card.

CHRISTMAS WINDOW

With the amount of cards given over the Christmas season it is nice to send something a little different, and this card will certainly stand out amongst the crowd. To decorate the miniature cards I have used sequins and small Christmas rubber stamps coloured with felt pens, but small stickers would look just as nice. You may like to write a short message in each one and these could even be personalized for each member of a family.

1. Glue the handmade paper onto the inside front flap of the card.

2. Trace template for the tree (to the dotted line only), cut one from black paper and glue into place onto the handmade paper. Add moonlight detail with the silver pen.

3. Draw round a coin on the silver card for the moon, cut out and glue onto the background.

4. Cut double-sided foam pads into smaller pieces and use to secure the front flap to the inside, behind the aperture, to give extra depth.

5. Cut a piece of tasselled braid to fit across the window and glue into place. With a spare strand, tie back the curtain at each side of the window and secure with a spot of glue. Glue the holly sequins to the top of the curtain.

6. Make several miniature cards and decorate as you like. Glue the cards to the window frame.

7. Add dots of glitter glue to the tree for 'lights'.

Double-fold card with window aperture and foil borderlines: card size 114 x 178mm (4½ x 7in), aperture 73 x 137mm (3 x 5¼in)

Handmade paper

Small quantity black paper for tree

Small piece of silver card and a silver pen

Short length of tasselled braid

Oddments of card to make miniature cards

Christmas sequins or stickers to decorate miniature cards

Glitter glue

Double-sided foam pads

About 1 hour

MOSAIC

This mosaic is very effective and has universal appeal. It is not difficult to make, just a little fiddly, but I think the effort is worth it. The easiest way to turn a picture into a mosaic, is to simply cut it into squares, and this method allows even complex pictures to be used. Another slightly more time-consuming approach, is to also cut around the detail within the picture, as I have done here, but for this method I would suggest selecting subjects with very simple shapes.

1 Carefully cut around the inner edge of the frame on the panel of wallpaper.

2 Trace template for the vase and cut one from gold paper or card.

3 Glue the vase onto the background. The glue must completely cover the back of the vase, or bits may tend to drop off as it is cut into squares, so I would recommend using spray adhesive.

4 Cut the picture into squares, these ones are approx. 10 x 10mm (³⁄₄ x ³⁄₄in). I would advise cutting your image into strips first, then one at a time, cut each strip into squares, keeping the pieces in order by laying them out in their correct positions on a spare sheet of paper, as you go.

5 Glue your mosaic onto the white card leaving small gaps between each piece. The gaps between the pieces need only be small to give a mosaic look, and slightly uneven spacing can actually add to the overall impression. It is easier to start with the centre strip and work out. It is better to use a large piece of card and to trim this afterwards, than to start with a piece that is too small.

6 Glue the finished mosaic onto the front of the card, then add the frame.

Single-fold card
150 x 203mm
(6 x 8in)

White card, large enough to hold your finished mosaic

Gold paper or card

Small panel cut from a roll of tile type wallpaper (using a panel from a roll of wallpaper has several advantages. It is quite thick, which helps with the mosaic appearance, the inner section has an interesting pattern, and it also has a ready-made frame).

About 1 hour

CHAPTER 9

Templates

ABOUT THE AUTHOR

Debbie Brown has been designing and making handmade cards for many years, initially for herself, then for friends and family, leading to commercial and commissioned sales both at home and abroad. She has had several articles published in craft magazines. She is married with two children and lives in Rickmansworth, Hertfordshire.

GMC Publications

BOOKS

CRAFTS

American Patchwork Designs in Needlepoint	
	Melanie Tacon
A Beginners' Guide to Rubber Stamping	*Brenda Hunt*
Blackwork: A New Approach	*Brenda Day*
Celtic Cross Stitch Designs	*Carol Phillipson*
Celtic Knotwork Designs	*Sheila Sturrock*
Celtic Knotwork Handbook	*Sheila Sturrock*
Celtic Spirals and Other Designs	*Sheila Sturrock*
Collage from Seeds, Leaves and Flowers	*Joan Carver*
Complete Pyrography	*Stephen Poole*
Contemporary Smocking	*Dorothea Hall*
Creating Colour with Dylon	*Dylon International*
Creative Doughcraft	*Patricia Hughes*
Creative Embroidery Techniques Using Colour Through Gold	
	Daphne J. Ashby & Jackie Woolsey
The Creative Quilter:	
Techniques and Projects	*Pauline Brown*
Decorative Beaded Purses	*Enid Taylor*
Designing and Making Cards	*Glennis Gilruth*
Glass Engraving Pattern Book	*John Everett*
Glass Painting	*Emma Sedman*
How to Arrange Flowers:	
A Japanese Approach to English Design	
	Taeko Marvelly
How to Make First-Class Cards	*Debbie Brown*
An Introduction to Crewel Embroidery	*Mave Glenny*
Making and Using Working Drawings	
for Realistic Model Animals	*Basil F. Fordham*
Making Character Bears	*Valerie Tyler*
Making Decorative Screens	*Amanda Howes*
Making Fairies and Fantastical Creatures	*Julie Sharp*
Making Greetings Cards for Beginners	*Pat Sutherland*
Making Hand-Sewn Boxes: Techniques	
and Projects	*Jackie Woolsey*
Making Knitwear Fit	*Pat Ashforth & Steve Plummer*
Making Mini Cards, Gift Tags & Invitations	
	Glennis Gilruth
Making Soft-Bodied Dough Characters	*Patricia Hughes*
Natural Ideas for Christmas:	
Fantastic Decorations to Make	
	Rosie Cameron-Ashcroft & Carol Cox
Needlepoint: A Foundation Course	*Sandra Hardy*
New Ideas for Crochet:	
Stylish Projects for the Home	*Darsha Capaldi*

Patchwork for Beginners	*Pauline Brown*
Pyrography Designs	*Norma Gregory*
Pyrography Handbook (Practical Crafts)	*Stephen Poole*
Ribbons and Roses	*Lee Lockheed*
Rose Windows for Quilters	*Angela Besley*
Rubber Stamping with Other Crafts	*Lynne Garner*
Sponge Painting	*Ann Rooney*
Stained Glass: Techniques and Projects	*Mary Shanahan*
Step-by-Step Pyrography Projects for	
the Solid Point Machine	*Norma Gregory*
Tassel Making for Beginners	*Enid Taylor*
Tatting Collage	*Lindsay Rogers*
Temari: A Traditional Japanese Embroidery Technique	
	Margaret Ludlow
Theatre Models in Paper and Card	*Robert Burgess*
Trip Around the World:	
25 Patchwork, Quilting and Appliqué Projects	
	Gail Lawther
Trompe l'Œil: Techniques and Projects	*Jan Lee Johnson*

WOODCARVING

The Art of the Woodcarver	*GMC Publications*
Carving Architectural Detail in Wood:	
The Classical Tradition	*Frederick Wilbur*
Carving Birds & Beasts	*GMC Publications*
Carving the Human Figure:	
Studies in Wood and Stone	*Dick Onians*
Carving Nature:	
Wildlife Studies in Wood	*Frank Fox-Wilson*
Carving Realistic Birds	*David Tippey*
Decorative Woodcarving	*Jeremy Williams*
Elements of Woodcarving	*Chris Pye*
Essential Woodcarving Techniques	*Dick Onians*
Further Useful Tips for Woodcarvers	*GMC Publications*
Lettercarving in Wood:	
A Practical Course	*Chris Pye*
Making & Using Working Drawings for Realistic	
Model Animals	*Basil F. Fordham*
Power Tools for Woodcarving	*David Tippey*
Practical Tips for Turners & Carvers	*GMC Publications*
Relief Carving in Wood:	
A Practical Introduction	*Chris Pye*
Understanding Woodcarving	*GMC Publications*

Understanding Woodcarving in the Round
GMC Publications

Useful Techniques for Woodcarvers   *GMC Publications*
Wildfowl Carving – Volume 1   *Jim Pearce*
Wildfowl Carving – Volume 2   *Jim Pearce*
Woodcarving: A Complete Course   *Ron Butterfield*
Woodcarving: A Foundation Course   *Zoë Gertner*
Woodcarving for Beginners   *GMC Publications*
Woodcarving Tools & Equipment Test Reports
GMC Publications

Woodcarving Tools, Materials & Equipment   *Chris Pye*

WOODTURNING

Adventures in Woodturning   *David Springett*
Bert Marsh: Woodturner   *Bert Marsh*
Bowl Turning Techniques Masterclass   *Tony Boase*
Colouring Techniques for Woodturners   *Jan Sanders*
Contemporary Turned Wood:
New Perspectives in a Rich Tradition
Ray Leier, Jan Peters & Kevin Wallace
The Craftsman Woodturner   *Peter Child*
Decorative Techniques for Woodturners   *Hilary Bowen*
Fun at the Lathe   *R.C. Bell*
Illustrated Woodturning Techniques   *John Hunnex*
Intermediate Woodturning Projects   *GMC Publications*
Keith Rowley's Woodturning Projects   *Keith Rowley*
Practical Tips for Turners & Carvers   *GMC Publications*
Turning Green Wood   *Michael O'Donnell*
Turning Miniatures in Wood   *John Sainsbury*
Turning Pens and Pencils
Kip Christensen & Rex Burningham
Understanding Woodturning   *Ann & Bob Phillips*
Useful Techniques for Woodturners   *GMC Publications*
Useful Woodturning Projects   *GMC Publications*
Woodturning: Bowls, Platters, Hollow Forms, Vases,
Vessels, Bottles, Flasks, Tankards, Plates
GMC Publications
Woodturning:
A Foundation Course (New Edition)   *Keith Rowley*
Woodturning: A Fresh Approach   *Robert Chapman*
Woodturning: An Individual Approach   *Dave Regester*
Woodturning: A Source Book of Shapes   *John Hunnex*
Woodturning Jewellery   *Hilary Bowen*
Woodturning Masterclass   *Tony Boase*
Woodturning Techniques   *GMC Publications*
Woodturning Tools & Equipment Test Reports
GMC Publications
Woodturning Wizardry   *David Springett*

WOODWORKING

Advanced Scrollsaw Projects   *GMC Publications*
Bird Boxes and Feeders for the Garden   *Dave Mackenzie*
Complete Woodfinishing   *Ian Hosker*

David Charlesworth's Furniture-Making Techniques
David Charlesworth
The Encyclopedia of Joint Making   *Terrie Noll*
Furniture & Cabinetmaking Projects   *GMC Publications*
Furniture-Making Projects for the Wood Craftsman
GMC Publications
Furniture-Making Techniques for the Wood Craftsman
GMC Publications
Furniture Projects   *Rod Wales*
Furniture Restoration (Practical Crafts)   *Kevin Jan Bonner*
Furniture Restoration and Repair for Beginners
Kevin Jan Bonner
Furniture Restoration Workshop   *Kevin Jan Bonner*
Green Woodwork   *Mike Abbott*

MAGAZINES

WOODTURNING ✦ WOODCARVING
FURNITURE & CABINETMAKING
THE ROUTER ✦ WOODWORKING
THE DOLLS' HOUSE MAGAZINE
WATER GARDENING ✦ EXOTIC
GARDENING ✦ GARDEN CALENDAR
OUTDOOR PHOTOGRAPHY
BLACK & WHITE PHOTOGRAPHY
BUSINESSMATTERS

The above represents a full list of all titles currently
published or scheduled to be published.
All are available direct from the Publishers or
through bookshops, newsagents and specialist
retailers.
To place an order, or to obtain a complete
catalogue, contact:

**GMC Publications,
Castle Place, 166 High Street, Lewes,
East Sussex BN7 1XU,
United Kingdom
Tel: 01273 488005
Fax: 01273 478606
E-mail: pubs@thegmcgroup.com**

Orders by credit card are accepted